THE
NIGHT
THE
MUSIC
ENDED

THE
NIGHT
THE
MUSIC
ENDED

BY
MARILYN BELLEMORE

The Merry Blacksmith Press
2012

The Night the Music Ended, The Station Nightclub:
March 2000 – February 2003

© 2012 Marilyn Bellemore

For information:

The Merry Blacksmith Press
70 Lenox Ave.
West Warwick, RI 02893

merryblacksmith.com

Published in the USA by The Merry Blacksmith Press

ISBN— 978-0-61573-202-2
0-61573-202-X

*This book is dedicated to the
victims and survivors of
The Station nightclub fire.*

TABLE OF CONTENTS

The poem "A Symbol of Hope" is engraved on a stone in the butterfly gardens at the Roger Williams Park Zoo in Providence, RI, dedicated to those affected by The Station nightclub fire. Photo by Marilyn Bellemore.

A Symbol of Hope

A butterfly lights beside us like a sunbeam
And for a brief moment its glory
and beauty belong to our world
But then it flies again
And though we wish it could have stayed...
We feel lucky to have seen it.

~ Unknown

Introduction

"Do you believe in rock 'n roll?"
                        – Don McLean, "American Pie"

ON FEBRUARY 20, 2003, my car broke down at a self service gas station off Thayer Street on the East Side of Providence, Rhode Island. It was around 8:30 p.m., and my plans were to attend the Great White concert at The Station nightclub in West Warwick that night.

Snow began to fall, and AAA Road Service told me not to expect to see them until after 10:30 p.m. I was furious. But, I waited and waited at the gas pump, all the while calling family and friends hoping to get a lift to the venue. No such luck.

When AAA finally arrived, it was well after 11 p.m., too late to attend the concert that would become the fourth deadliest fire in American nightclub history.

For two years, beginning in 2000, I was a journalist at the *Kent County Daily Times* in West Warwick. To liven up my beat, I covered rock concerts at The Station nightclub. I was one of the few reporters in the state that wrote about the bands that played there. West Warwick was considered by many to be a run-down, predominantly low income, mill town. Therefore, this nightclub and the music that was played there was not of much interest to the big city journalists.

The prevailing thought was that a good many has-been bands or never-were bands played at The Station. But, this wasn't necessarily the case. Among the groups that performed there were international acts that had followings. In the course of my work, I would see and hear some of the hottest musicians of the 1970s and 80s. I had many great interviews, and the articles appeared in the *Kent County Daily Times,* in advance of the show. Since my writing was then finished, I would frequently go to the nightclub to enjoy the show, just as a spectator.

The Station nightclub was pretty obscure, and wasn't widely known outside that part of Rhode Island. Even so, it would draw an audience from neighboring states if the particular bands had a broader appeal. Then, in the course of one night, The Station became the best known club in the state for the worst reasons.

I walked through the doors of the nightclub just about every week or two to drop off copies of articles I had written or attend a concert or fundraiser. Even after I left my job at the newspaper, I'd still stop in to say hello to staff members or catch a show.

During my years as a journalist, I wrote for several newspapers in Rhode Island, and I interviewed hun-

The Station nightclub tickets, top from 2002 and bottom from 2003.
Courtesy of Tom Lanigan who played with Bonnis Herd.

dreds of people in the music industry including Ted Nugent, The J. Geils Band, The Commitments, photographer Henry Diltz (Under the Covers: A Magical Journey), Staind, Joe Perry, Fred Durst (Limp Bizkit), Eddie Money, and Rick Derringer. It was an eclectic mix of artists and gave me the opportunity to go to concerts at a variety of venues in Rhode Island and Massachusetts, my favorite being The Station nightclub.

I could go there alone and feel safe and comfortable. I'd sit at the bar or in the back of the dance floor and watch concertgoers rock out with the bands. There was always a constant flow of people. It was a fun, friendly atmosphere.

At the end of the night, I looked forward to going to the backstage room to introduce myself to the musicians with whom I had done the telephone interviews. It was a tiny space where the performers could rest before and after the shows. On the walls were two guitars which were routinely signed by the people who played there.

These were the golden times at The Station. Before that tragic night, for many fans of particular types of music, it was the go-to place in southern New England. This book more references those happy years, leaving the in depth coverage of the tragedy and its aftermath to other authors.

A portion of the proceeds of this book will go to The Station Fire Memorial Foundation to help construct and maintain a permanent memorial at the site of the former nightclub. What follows is the story of The Station and that catastrophic night, intermixed with a collection of newspaper articles highlighting some of the music and good times. The news items are presented in their entirety with the permission of *The Kent County Daily Times*.

Marilyn Bellemore
2012

A Brief History of
The Station Nightclub

*"And I knew if I had my chance That I could
make these people dance And maybe they'd be
happy for a while."*
– Don McLean, "American Pie"

When brothers Henry and Casimir "Casey" Lada
bought a cornfield at 211 Cowesctt Ave. on Nov. 21,
1945, the village of Arctic, across the town in West Warwick, was the center where clothing stores and eateries
thrived. Perhaps the Ladas hoped for similar success in
this small village of Crompton, because the following
summer, they opened Casey's on the site. This nightspot
promised dining and dancing with orchestra music on
Friday and Saturday nights.

Along with the business, the brothers were active in
local sports. Henry was the star second baseman in the
Pawtuxet Valley Sunday Baseball League (PVSBL) for St.
James as well as a basketball player at Falcon Hall. Casey

excelled as the first basemen for the Old Red Bridge Tigers and then for the senior team in Crompton. This team won many championships in the PVSBL and the Pawtuxet Valley Twilight Baseball League.

But, for one reason or another, on March 25, 1947, Casey Lada sued his brother Henry in Superior Court and gave up his share of the business. Less than three months later, Henry renamed it The Wheel. It became a major hangout for Navy sailors from Quonset Point in North Kingstown.

Donald Carpenter, 73, a West Warwick native and local historian, remembers The Wheel when he was a young boy. Carpenter, a past president of the Pawtuxet Valley Preservation and Historical Society, said that in the early 1900s, Cowesett Avenue was primarily agricultural. With the advent of the automobile and newer roads, it soon became the main road to New York.

"I think the major thing is the shift from agricultural to commercial on Cowesett Avenue," said Carpenter. "By 1960, we saw a shift in commercialism. The center of West Warwick had been Arctic. The main shift went to the Rhode Island Mall in Warwick and Cowesett Avenue with the building of strip stores."

In 1964, Henry Lada sold The Wheel, and from that point on, it flipped through a series of owners and name changes.

Here's a breakdown of the ensuing years:

- June 10, 1964: The Wheel is sold to Local 1350, American Federation of State, County and Municipal Employees which used it as a meeting hall known as Club 1350.

- May 12, 1967: Joseph P. Muschiano buys the club and names it Cedar Acres.

- Circa 1968: Muschiano renames it The Doll House.

- April 27, 1970: Charles E. and Jeanne L. Petrarca buy the club and call it Red Fox Inn.

- Later 1970: The Petrarcas change the name to Tammany Hall.

- June 9, 1971: Greater Providence Trust Co. takes over the land after the Petrarcas default on their mortgage.

- November 1, 1971: Michael Muksian and Robert Pariseault buy the club and call it Julio's.

- March 21, 1972: A suspicious fire damages the club. A week before, the name on the liquor license had been changed to the Red Baron Inn.

- June 5, 1974: Triton Industries, controlled by Raymond J. Villanova, buys the club and opens P. Brillo & Sons.

- February 5, 1985: Brillo's liquor license is transferred to Glenn M. Madden, former Brillo's manager, who renames it Glenn's Pub.

- 1991: Kenik Corporation, owned by Nicholas R. DeChristofaro and managed by Kenneth G. Ucci, reopens the club as CrackerJacks.

- January 5, 1993: Cracker-Jacks liquor license is transferred to Raymond P. "Skip" Shogren, who renames the club The Filling Station.

The Filling Station

211 Cowesett Avenue, West Warwick, RI
823-4060

- December 5, 1995: The liquor license is transferred to Howard J. Julian, who continues to call it The Filling Station.

On March 21, 2000, the business called The Filling Station is sold to Michael and Jeffrey Derderian who re-name it The Station. When it burns down three years later, this

Sign outside The Station on February 15, 2001.
Photo courtesy of Rich Antonelli.

modest roadhouse structure, which had been a venue for everything from big band orchestra music to hard rock, had curiously begun and ended its tenure under the ownership of a pair of brothers.

Thursday, July 20, 2000
THE TUBES ROLL INTO THE STATION ON SATURDAY

– Marilyn Bellemore, Daily Times Staff Reporter

THE TUBES are about to please everybody, including their fans from the '70s and '80s. And they just might gain some new followers.

In support of its brand new album, the group will be landing at The Station in West Warwick on Saturday night to play some favorites, old and new.

"We're just doing four or five shows on the East Coast," said Fee Waybill, lead singer. "We're just doing sporadic shows until our new record comes out."

The Tubes World Tour 2000 will be available on Oct. 3.

"This new one is a quasi-live record," explained Waybill. "We started with a live per-

The Tubes, 2001.

formance. In the old days, people used to say we were a great live band, but couldn't catch it on tape. So, we started with a live track with live drums. We fixed, changed, and added stuff from a live basis."

"In addition, we have new studio tracks. One was a reunion with David Foster who produced our old hits. That came out great! We've signed to a real record company now called CMC records. They're primarily a classic rock label. They're a big label and have real distribution, a real publicity staff, and promotional staff."

Until the record release, The Tubes have been going out over the weekend and doing two or three shows.

"In the summer, there are too many bands out there," said Waybill.

In 1986, Waybill left The Tubes. The group got back together in 1994, and in 1996 came *Genius of America*, its first release in 10 years.

"It was new material on a small independent label called Popular Records," said Waybill. "They went out of business and didn't widely distribute the record."

In 1999, *Dawn of The Tubes* was released.

"It's ancient materials from the '70s that was owned by an engineer," said Waybill. "He sold the tapes to a company that specializes in that (type of thing). It's kind of wacky and interesting. It's an old two-track tape. We couldn't really go in and mix anything."

Waybill reported that, including himself, four out of the seven original members of The Tubes will be appearing at The Station. Roger Steen will be on guitar, Prairie Prince on drums, and Rick Anderson on bass.

Additions to the band are Gary Cambra on guitar and keyboards, David Medd on synthesizer, and female vocalist Lesley Paton.

"When we got back together, we did it as a hobby," said Waybill. "Roger (Steen) is a distributor for ABC. Rick (Anderson) owns a used car lot, and I'm a songwriter. I write and publish songs. Doing Tubes gigs is kind of a side job.

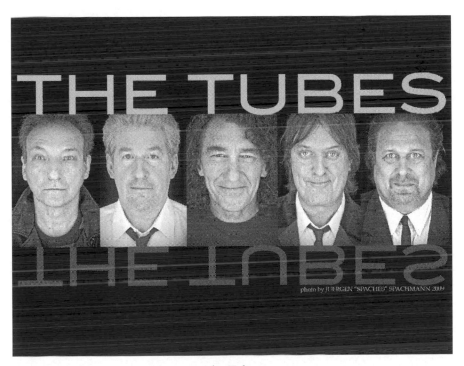

The Tubes.

"It's all starting to get real again. (We're) going to go out on a tour this fall in a hideous bus and kill ourselves... and then Europe in the spring."

Will you get to hear the old Tubes hits at The Station on Saturday night?

"Absolutely," said Waybill. "'She's a Beauty,' 'Talk to Ya Later,' 'White Punks on Dope,' 'Sushi Girl,' and 'Mondo Bondage' as well as new stuff. There's no getting around it. It's what people want to hear.

"We're going to do a show like we used to with costumes. The whole nine yards ...maybe not nine but maybe seven and a half."

The Sherman Oaks, Calif. resident is originally from Arizona.

"I started as a roadie for Roger's (Steen) band," said Waybill. "The Tubes were a combination of two bands. When the two bands merged together, I kind of started as a background singer."

And what we all want to know is, how do you go from John to Fee?

"Fee was shortened from Fiji, like the country, the island," explained Waybill. "For some reason someone in the band thought I kind of looked like the King of Fiji. He was on an old *National Geographic* cover... That was around 1975."

The Tubes will be at The Station this Saturday, July 22 at 11 p.m. Tickets are $16. Opening acts start at

8:30 p.m. and include The Complaints and White Collar Criminals.

Blue Oyster Cult was supposed to be the first band I interviewed that played at The Station. The group cancelled its performance at the last minute. Turns out, my "debut" was with The Tubes. What stuck out in my mind was the MTV video for the 1983 single "She's a Beauty." It was a little raunchy, and I was a bit too shy to ask Fee Waybill how it came to be because he was my first celebrity interview.

In the video, a young boy (who later became Alexis Arquette, the trans woman actress/musician) takes a carnival ride sitting on the lap of a dominatrix. He bounces up and down on her as they go through scenes of women dressed in provocative outfits such as a mermaid, trapeze artist, and cavewoman.

In a YouTube performance in June 2008, Fee Waybill explained he got the idea to co-write the song when he was outside a massage parlor in San Francisco. There was a kiosk with a sign that read "Talk to A Naked Girl for A Dollar." The woman inside wore a bra and panties, and he ended up paying three dollars to be aggravated.

The Tubes are still actively performing. The website is www.thetubes.com.

Honeymoon Suite, August 19, 2000. Lead guitarist Derry Grehan on left; lead singer Johnnie Dee on right. Photo by Marilyn Bellemore.

With Derry Grehan, lead guitar player for Honeymoon Suite (left) and other band members, August 19, 2000.

Thursday, Aug. 17, 2000
HONEYMOON SUITE BRINGS 1980s STYLE MELODIC ROCK INTO THE FUTURE

– Marilyn Bellemore, Daily Times Staff Reporter

THEY MAY BE A PRODUCT of the 1980s, but this band is certainly not living there.

Honeymoon Suite, best known for hits like "Feel It Again," "New Girl Now," and "Burning in Love," will be at The Station on Cowesett Avenue in West Warwick this Saturday night. Although it is one of a group of bands made popular in the '80s playing at The Station this summer, the members of Honeymoon Suite said they intend to establish themselves as something more in the new millennium.

"I don't know what's going on," explained Johnnie Dee, lead vocalist, about the sudden revival In '80s music. "Because we came out in the '80s doesn't mean we're stuck in '80s music. The band has always been playing consistently. We come out as naturally as we possibly can. We try to get our songs across, no bull or posing."

Dee, a singer/songwriter from Niagara Falls, Ontario, Canada, originally began in bands as a lead guitar player when he was 14.

17

"I started Honeymoon Suite when I was 21 and it was like a bar band," said Dee, who never had a single voice lesson, but credits his vocal ability to proper breathing. "We'd been playing for six months when I met Derry Grehan (lead guitar). It wasn't too long before we knew we had a record deal."

The Niagara Falls area's popularity as a honeymoon destination is the origin of the group's name.

Grehan, also from the Niagara Falls area, the town of St. Catharines, Ontario, started playing guitar when he was around 11 years old.

"I just did what every other kid did," said Grehan. "Played my guitar pretty much. I always wanted to be in a band. Johnnie and I come from the same place, but we never really knew each other until we met in Toronto.

"Johnnie already had Honeymoon Suite going. We had the same agent who ended up becoming our manager. I had a gig and said, 'do you know bands that need a guitar player?' The agent turned me on to Honeymoon Suite for an audition around 1982."

Grehan said that Dee is the voice and he is the guitar player. Grehan writes most of the songs although he and Dee have collaborated on many.

"Songwriting is a result of playing guitar," said Grehan, who generalizes the band's sound as melodic rock. "It was the next step for me. It's whatever comes out (at the moment)."

Honeymoon Suite's *Racing After Midnight* album cover from 1988.
Permission of Derry Grehan.

In 1984, their first album, *Honeymoon Suite* was released. The group became an instant sensation with the hits "New Girl Now" and "Burning in Love."

The Big Prize followed in 1986 and with it came the popular "Feel It Again" and "What Does It Take."

The group's last studio album, *Monsters Under the Bed*, came in 1992. And the album, *13 Live*, was released in 1994.

"People always thought we broke up," said Grehan. "We were always playing, but not as much. I miss playing in the States. It's important for us."

Honeymoon Suite's latest project is a brand new CD which it finished recording a month or two ago. The band is looking forward to an autumn release date and, although it is not yet titled, Dee said he thinks *Touch the Sun* is a possibility.

The group has management located in Chicago, so the album may be released on an American label.

Honeymoon Suite still maintains a following. Many websites have been dedicated to the band with one as far away as Sweden.

As for Saturday night's performance, Dee said he wants to get up and sing and make everyone happy.

"We're going to try to play as much music as we can Saturday night," said Dee. "At a lot of outdoor festivals, we have to stop because of sound curfews. But, inside a club we don't. We have so much music; you can expect a high energy show."

"We're going to play all the best old songs and songs from the new record as well," added Grehan.

The band has opened for groups like Heart and ZZ Top in the past. But, Saturday's show in West Warwick is all theirs.

"The Station is going to be a fun place to come to," said Grehan. "We haven't been to Rhode Island in a long time."

Expect to hear Peter Nunn on keyboards, Brett Carrigan on drums, and Rob Laidlaw on bass.

"This is our show, and we're going to play live and natural," said Dee.

Tickets for Honeymoon Suite are $9 in advance and $11 the day of the show. $kyhigh and The Com plaints open the night.

I was a college student when Honeymoon Suite hit the music scene, and, at that time, I was following bands like U2, Dire Straits, and R.E.M. Still, I knew the song "What Does It Take" was featured in the closing credits of the 1986 film "One Crazy Summer" starring John Cusack. I also remember Honeymoon Suite won a Juno Award for Group of the Year in 1986.

With Johnnie Dee, lead singer for the Canadian rock band
Honeymoon Suite, on August 19, 2000.

I decided to see the band play because my cousin, Melanie, was a huge fan, and I thought it would be nice to get her an autograph. I went with my on-again, off-again boyfriend to the concert, and he managed to get a cassette tape of Honeymoon Suite's The Big Prize, *from his brother for the band to sign.*

Backstage, we hung out with the guys for a while.

Two days later, when I was at my desk in the newsroom, I got a call from Johnnie Dee who was back in Ontario. He was interested in getting some photos I had taken of the band playing at The Station. Much to my surprise, I found myself packing a suitcase, grabbing my passport, and heading for the Canadian border.

Honeymoon Suite still tours and puts out CDs (www.honeymoonsuite.com).

Thursday, August 24, 2000
THE OUTFIELD GOES TO BAT AT THE STATION

– Marilyn Bellemore, Daily Times Staff Reporter

IF YOU GRADUATED MORE THAN a decade ago and you're yearning for your younger days, you might want to catch The Outfield on Wed., Aug 30 at The Station on Cowesett Avenue.

"People like to hang around with their high school past," said Tony Lewis, lead vocalist. "We feel we have timeless music. It sounds good in any year. We weren't a band that sold for image. We're good live... the best three-piece band around."

The band's latest CD, *Extra Innings*, is already proving to be a success.

"The response has been excellent, encouraging," said guitarist John Spinks. "Twenty-one and 22-year-olds, a generation down, now seem to enjoy the same kind of music."

Spinks, the son of a piano player, said he first became interested in guitar when he was five or six years old.

"It wasn't really a guitar," said Spinks. "It was a tennis racket. The beat came along, and I was very young. I tried to emulate by putting on strings to make it sound like a guitar. I watched TV and tried to impersonate. I wanted to be in a band when most children wanted to be a football or soccer player."

Spinks, who grew up in the east end of London, said he got his start when he was 12 with a bunch of kids at Susan Lawrence Primary School. A central theme of his songwriting is about life and relating.

"I was singing Police songs one night," said Lewis. "John (Spinks) came and saw us that night and said 'why don't you sing like that all the time?' Normally, I sang music in a lower key, but he said my voice sounds better when I sing higher."

The Outfield.

Spinks, who now resides in Kent County, England, wrote songs for Lewis to sing. Lewis credits Spinks for recognizing something he could do that he didn't see himself.

Lewis said he and Spinks began playing cover songs in various pubs. Music like the Beatles, Rolling Stones, Albatross, and the Eagles.

The group's original name came from a street gang, the Baseball Boys, in the movie "The Warriors" (1979).

"The band was called the Baseball Boys," said Lewis. "John wrote the songs in the studio. Alan (Jackman, the original drummer) and myself were asked to do some sessions. What started off as a project ended up being something bigger.

"When American management got interested, they said we couldn't use the name Baseball Boys. It would be like Chinese noodles to the Chinese. These are three guys in the outfield, so that was it."

The Outfield came to America in 1985 with the release of its first album *Play Deep*.

"Our first single, 'Say It Isn't So,' did well in regions, but not nationally," said Lewis. "'Your Love' had a slow momentum, but by the time we got to America, it was a big hit at number five. It's a song that's just got legs; it doesn't burn out."

Over the next seven years, the group's albums, titled

with baseball overtones, offered a string of hits.

Bangin', released in 1987, included "Since You've Been Gone" and "No Surrender." *Voices of Babylon* came in 1989, and the song of the same name became an instant hit as did "The Night Ain't Over."

One of the band's best known hits was "For You" which appeared on its 1990 album *Diamond Days*.

Three compilations, *Playing the Field* (1992), *Big Innings: Best of the Outfield* (1996), and *Super Hits* (1998) followed.

Lewis, who now lives in Hertfordshire, outside of London, said that although the band is technically English, it's an American product.

"We can't even get arrested in England," joked the lead vocalist. "When we were popular in America, the music in England was more novelty songs kids under five would sing. It was a privilege for us to be off the charts there. We didn't want to compete with puppets.

"After 1992, when grunge took over, we took a back seat," said Lewis. "We thought people may have overdosed."

Lewis explained that The Outfield has a big fan in Danny Roberts, from Atlanta, GA, who dedicated a website in its honor. The gentleman's wife contacted the band in 1998, and it is now its official information bureau. Check it out at www.theoutfield.com.

"The thing we find so sad is that stations that played our kind of music, it doesn't matter to them anymore," said Spinks. "We wish we could go back to that time. It's the generation of people ages 25 to 35 that gets overlooked."

The Outfield. Left to right: John Spinks, Tony Lewis, and Alan Jackman.

Spinks added that the band's release *It Ain't Over* (1998) is now a collector's item because only 2000 copies were produced.

The Outfield reappeared in September 1998 when it played along with Rick Springfield and Howard Jones.

"We were going to play a few shows," said Lewis. "It ended up being 55 shows!"

The band is still popular in Trinidad and many parts of South America.

Surprisingly, Lewis' British accent is not so pronounced in his singing voice.

"Eric Clapton said something like you can't sing English," said Lewis. "I can't sing the way I talk or I'll sound like Julie Andrews."

The group finishes up a six-week tour in mid-September and then heads back to England for Christmas.

At Wednesday's show, Simon Dawson will be on drums, replacing Jackman. The band promises to play old favorites.

"There will also be stuff from *Extra Innings*," added Spinks.

Tickets for The Outfield are $16 in advance and $18 the day of the show. The opening acts are White Collar Criminals and Mill City Rockers.

"We're here a few days early. We want to hit some West Warwick watering holes, and we'd like you to be our guide," said a British voice from the other end of the receiver.

During my days as a journalist, I received phone calls that ranged from an anonymous death threat for revealing where the gravestone of alleged West Greenwich vampire Nellie Vaughn was hidden to a call from a woman who was held at gunpoint and contacted me first before summoning the West Warwick Police. But, I never received a phone call asking me to be someone's drinking buddy.

Tony Lewis wanted me to give The Outfield the low-down on what bars to visit in town. Most anyone would have jumped at the chance to have a beer, or two, or three with the guys who made "Your Love" famous. I was either trying to maintain some form of professionalism or it was that I wasn't much of a drinker. So, I declined his offer.

When I got off the phone, an editor, who overheard the conversation, was flabbergasted.

"What? You said 'no?'" she asked.

We laugh about it to this day.

The Outfield still performs. The official website is www.theoutfield.com.

The Station and the Community

"A long, long time ago I can still remember how
that music used to make me smile"
      – Don McLean, "American Pie"

BY THE JUNE 2000, The Station was fast becoming a top venue in the state to hear internationally recognized heavy metal and rock acts. It was also a place where local musicians could open for bands like Cinderella, Sebastian Bach, Warrant, and Slaughter and headline on other nights.

"The atmosphere was unique. It felt like a local pub, warm and friendly. Yet, the stage and sound was set up like a rock concert," recalled Dean Petrella, 39, lead singer with The Complaints. "We played with a lot of great bands there. To name a few, Dave Davies of The Kinks, 10,000 Maniacs, and The Tubes."

Petrella, who lives less than two miles from where The Station was located in West Warwick, performed there dozens of times and was there hundreds of times as a patron.

"Nothing has been able to replace the nightclub since," he said. "It is greatly missed."

Rich Antonelli, 41, of Greenville, said if he wasn't playing at The Station with his former band $kyhigh and opening for bands like Honeymoon Suite and Quiet Riot, he could still be found there passing out flyers for his band's next show.

"It was close to where I lived in Cranston and had a lot of the bands I grew up with that other venues wouldn't touch anymore," Antonelli said.

$kyhigh played at many of the benefit concerts at The Station including one for 9/11. The last time the band

In front of Warrant's tour bus at The Station. Left to right:
Frank Soltys ($kyhigh), Erik Turner (Warrant), Rich Antonelli ($kyhigh),
Jerry Dixon (Warrant), Steve Carnevale ($kyhigh).
Photo courtesy of Rich Antonelli.

performed at the nightclub was in September 2002. Antonelli said that he had a falling out with one of the owners over the band's pay one night.

"Sometimes things happen for a reason," he said.

Antonelli also designed the website for The Station and updated and maintained it. He took this job when Howard Julian was the owner and continued it with the Derderians.

"Jeff (Derderian) called me to take down the website around 9 a.m. (the morning after the fire)," Antonelli said. "I never heard from them again."

Today, Antonelli plays guitar in a Bon Jovi tribute band called Bon Jersey, and he is working on his first solo album that will be called "Voiccless." It's all instrumental, and proceeds will go to the gastroenterology department at Hasbro Children's Hospital in Providence to advance the cure of Crohn's disease. He expects the CD to be released in early 2013.

"It's been 10 years since it all happened and longer than that since I was in the place," said Antonelli. "I'm just grateful my band never played there again after that night in September and wish the best for those that survived."

Tom Lanigan, 35, of Warwick, who played with the band Screaming Under Stars, referred to The Station as his second home.

"We were an up and coming band. We were excited about the opportunities to play there and be a part of the scene," said Lanigan. "The atmosphere was laid back. We were a young band hanging out in a friendly environment."

The Dublin, Ireland native lived in Scituate, Rhode Island during the time he first played at The Station. The last two years the nightclub was in operation, Lanigan

Tom Lanigan of the Tom Lanigan Band. Photo by Gene Carpenter.

performed with a band called Bonnis Herd every Tuesday and on alternate weekends.

"One of the strangest things was the night before it burnt down, they gave us tickets to go to the Great White concert so we could give out free drink passes for our show that was the following weekend." remembered Lanigan. "We were literally on our way there, but we had a show a couple of days later and we weren't prepared for it. We decided to rehearse, instead."

One of Lanigan's best friends, Eric, was a huge Great White fan. The concert was sold out, and a few comp tickets were left. Lanigan was able to secure Eric a place on the guest list.

"I remember his car was snowed in," said Lanigan, who was Eric's next door neighbor, "We helped him push his car out of the snow."

Eric made it to the Great White concert and died in the fire. He was one of the last bodies found, according to Lanigan.

"My heart was broken," said Lanigan, who performed at one of the big benefits immediately following the fire. "The Station was one of those places I'll always remember. Unfortunately, we lost a lot of great people that night. At the same time, I have a lot of fondness for the place…my memory of that time period. It was just really special."

Thursday, September 28, 2000
THE STATION HOSTS SAMANTHA 7, WITH POISON ROCKER C.C. DEVILLE, THIS WEEK

– Marilyn Bellemore, Daily Times Staff Reporter

NOW THAT THE POISON is out of his system, C.C. DeVille has returned to life as a lead singer in a new band.

Samantha 7 will be at The Station, 211 Cowesett Ave., on Wednesday, Oct. 4 to perform music from its self-titled debut album.

"It's a brand new CD, a departure from the Poison stuff," said DeVille, 36, lead guitarist for the band. "It's almost a success story in itself. Here's a guy that actually went through the pitfalls of rock & roll—drugs, drinking, girls—and the thing is now to have another chance at it. I'm singing now, and my life has turned 180 degrees."

DeVille said that when he was first in Poison, his

C. C. DeVille.

life was desperate and bleak. He said he got so down and so low. But, now things have changed.

"I finally have something to say after all these years," said DeVille. "I know what I'm doing now. I had the success at a young age, but I didn't know what to do with the success. The positive side you need to put into perspective. Life goes on. By getting back up, it's been inspirational for people around me as well. I'm so proud of it. It's amazing there was a story."

The Brooklyn native became widely recognized as the lead guitar player for Poison from the mid 1980s through the early 1990s. The band's album *Look What the Cat Dragged In* (1986) went triple platinum with such hits as "Talk Dirty to Me" and "I Won't Forget You." The five times platinum *Open Up and Say... Ahh!* (1988) included the gold #1 hit "Every Rose Has Its Thorn" and also the popular "Fallen Angel" and "Nothin' But a Good Time."

The release of *Flesh & Blood* (1990) was triple platinum and included two gold hits "Something to Believe In" and "Unskinny Bop" as well as "Ride the Wind" and "Life Goes On."

"There is so much more meaning to my life than before," said the Los Angeles resident. "I've been clean and sober for five years. I wrote all the songs on this album. I wrote a majority of the songs on Poison records. This is the first time I'm singing. It gives a whole new dimension."

DeVille said he became a singer out of desperation. There was no one to sing his songs, so he took over the reigns.

"That desperation fuels me," said DeVille. "(The lyrics) it's basically life history. It's a real record. The songs are like my children. I love them all for different reasons. I guarantee you'll love it; you'll go through it fast. The album is doing well."

The lead singer named his band, which includes Krys Baratto (bass, vocals) and Francis Ruiz (drums, vocals), Samantha 7 for a favorite childhood cartoon. The group's manager is Ron DeBlasio, a Providence native, born on Federal Hill and raised in Silver Lake.

C.C. DeVille (Getty Images).

This tour, which kicked off on Sept. 22 and will run for two months, is the first solo tour for DeVille and Samantha 7.

Despite his lows with Poison, DeVille remains lead guitar player for the band and toured with Poison this summer.

$kyhigh will open Wednesday night's Station show. Tickets are $9 in advance and $11 the day of the show.

C.C. DeVille didn't do a lot interviews, and he actually claimed to have "come out" during this interview. This great revelation, my scoop as it were, was his admissions about drugs, alcohol, and chasing women. It was amusing, and I was somewhat flattered that he opened up to me. But, this hardly put me on my way to being a good journalist.

Samantha 7 broke up in 2004. Ty Longley, a guitarist, played for a time in the band. He later died as a member of Great White in The Station nightclub fire.

Poison is still an active band. Its official site is www.poisonweb.com.

Thursday, October 5, 2000
NRBQ BRINGS MIX OF SOUND
TO STATION

– Marilyn Bellemore, Daily Times Staff Reporter

THEY HAVE A MUSICAL HISTORY that spans more than three decades, and they're still going strong.

NRBQ will bring its official brand of rock & roll to The Station, 211 Cowesett Ave., on Saturday night.

"I'd say we play a lot of different kind of styles," said Joey Spampinato, bass player. "We came up with a title called omni-pop. We're basically a rock & roll band, pop music, jazz, so many different things. If I said one thing I wouldn't be accurate."

The band members first met in Florida in 1967. He and keyboardist Terry Adams were playing in two different bands at the time, Spampinato said. Adams' band was called NRBQ. Adams played piano with them, but it didn't last long.

"They disbanded temporarily," said Spampinato. "So, we played for a few months, then we disbanded. We put together what was NRBQ to go on and record. We came to New York, got signed to Columbia Records, and recorded toward the end of 1968. The

41

NRBQ promotional photo.

album (titled *NRBQ*) came out in February 1969."

From there, it did another album for Columbia, *Boppin' the Blues*, then moved to Kama Sutra around 1972. After two albums with them, NRBQ started its own label, Red Rooster. Subsequently, it recorded the well-known *At Yankee Stadium* with Mercury Records.

"We kind of combined with Red Rooster and Rounder in 1979," said Spampinato, a Nashville resident. "We've had an ongoing relationship with Rounder Records. In 1997, (we) put out a children's CD, *You're Nice People You Are*. A friend thought we'd make a good children's album. Every once in a while we put out a song that someone might think it's a children's one. We never thought of it as a children's idea."

The bass player said the album did pretty well although he doesn't know how many sold. He said

NRBQ would like to reintroduce it into the children's section of a record store because it never was officially listed and stocked there.

"We all take part in it (writing)," said Spampinato. "Me and Terry most, Johnny some. I wrote half of them. On that particular one, I wrote more. Musically, I don't change anything. I didn't necessarily think of them as children's songs. It's the way I feel that day. When we were growing up, music was so simplified. Now, it's almost playing down to the kids."

Spampinato said that all the members of NRBQ have never done anything else. Since its beginning, the band went through a drummer change in 1974 when Tom Ardolino joined. The most recent change was his brother Johnny Spampinato on guitar for six and a half years replacing Al Anderson.

"A lot of people like us to play the older songs," said Spampinato. "It's always different. We know what

NRBQ promotional photo.

NRBQ promotional photo.

we're going to play for the first song and then from there we see what needs to be played judging by what bounces back off the people. When we go on stage, we're playing for the moment. We may do something off our very first album at Saturday's show."

Although NRBQ hasn't had a release in a year, the band has something exciting in store.

"There's going to be a release," said Spampinato. "(We) put out an album in 1972 (called) *Scraps*. This is a *Scraps* companion, and it will be out in a month or two."

Shady Neighbors and Screaming Under Stars will open Saturday night. Tickets for NRBQ are $10 in advance and $12 the day of the show.

Of all the bands I interviewed that played at The Station, NRBQ was the only one I was not quite familiar with. However, I did know the tunes "Me and the Boys" and "Ridin' in My Car" as performed by other musicians. NRBQ more frequently played in Providence at Lupo's Heartbreak Hotel. Several members of the band appeared in the movie Complex World *which was filmed in Providence, the capitol city to the north of West Warwick.*

Today, Joey Spampinato is no longer with NRBQ, and now plays in the Spampinato Brothers with his brother, Johnny. Terry Adams announced he had stage four throat cancer in 1994. He is still with the band. Tom Ardolino, longtime drummer, died on January 6, 2012.

For the latest NRBQ concert dates, go to www. nrbq.com.

The Fire

"We all got up to dance, oh, but we never got
the chance."
　　　　　　　　　　– Don McLean, "American Pie"

"AS SOON AS THE PYRO WENT OFF, I saw it catching on the walls, and Jack Russell (the lead singer) threw a drink at the fire," recalled Chris Blacklock, 48, of Middletown. "I said 'this f—king place is on fire. We have to get out of here.'"

Blacklock, who had been to The Station nightclub dozens of times to hear bands like Anthrax, Raven, Fates Warning, and Savatage, was at the Great White concert with his girlfriend, Patti Clarke, 48, also of Middletown. Just a few months earlier, the couple had seen Jack Russell perform solo at Jared's Place, a small club in Attleboro, Mass.

Earlier on the night of the Great White concert, Blacklock and Clarke enjoyed a leisurely dinner at Out-

47

Jack Russell and Great White.

back Steakhouse in Warwick. He had a beer or two and she, a Mike's Hard Lemonade.

"That day, we were deciding should we or shouldn't we go to The Station," explained Clarke. "Chris's dad had just died the week before. And I said 'he would want you to go and live your life.'"

When they got to the nightclub, Blacklock noticed many unfamiliar faces and lots of drunkenness. The couple spoke to some acquaintances and listened to an opening band. Blacklock grabbed a beer and, Clarke, a water. It was her second time at The Station.

"Even if you didn't know people by name, they were really friendly," Blacklock recalled. "These were people who generally liked the same type of music. There were always good bands. It was kind of like a little family."

At 11 pm, Clarke made her way to the ladies room, near a dead end corridor. When she returned three min utes later, Blacklock was where she had left him, by the kitchen "take out" window in the main room.

It was only seconds into Great White's opening song "Desert Moon," at 11:07 p.m., that pyrotechnics set off by Daniel Biechele, the group's tour manager, started the fire.

At first, many patrons thought the flames were part of the act. But, as the fire reached the ceiling and smoke began to billow, they realized the situation was out of control.

Blacklock and Clarke tried to exit the building through the main entrance, but they saw a crowd was forming and effectively blocking the front doors. Black-lock remembered there was an exit in the adjoining room, near the horseshoe-shaped bar. So, he yelled that out loud, and many people followed him in that direc-tion seeking an alternate exit.

As they made their way toward the door, Clarke, petite in size, gripped Blacklock's leather jacket. When Blacklock, six-foot-one and 245 pounds, reached the exit, he thought his jacket was stuck (not realizing it was Clarke) and broke free into the cold February night.

Survivors Patti Clarke and Chris Blacklock.

The door slammed shut, with Clarke left behind. She estimated she was inside the burning building for another 45 seconds. In the darkness, she heard glass from light bulbs and liquor bottles cracking, and people screaming. She looked back and saw a man in a gray hooded sweatshirt. He pushed her to safety through the door, and Clarke landed on her knees in a snowbank.

"And as the flames climbed high into the night"
                                        – Don McLean, "American Pie"

"It was like a war zone," said Clarke. "Everyone was running around. There was chaos and pandemonium."

Blacklock had already called 911, and the couple spent the next several hours helping survivors to ambulances or gently assisting the wounded who were throwing their burned bodies into the snow to relieve the pain.

"It was a disaster no one knew was going to happen," said Blacklock. "No one was prepared for it. It's nothing you want to see or want anyone else to see."

Blacklock attributes his survival during the fourth deadliest nightclub fire in American history to luck, his familiarity with the layout of the building, and his ability to react quickly.

"As days go by, I try to put it behind me, but something will spark a memory," he added, nearly 10 years later. "It's something you'll never forget."

Although Blacklock and Clarke had never met Major Mark Knott, 42, of the West Warwick Police Department, Knott, too, was at The Station on the night of the tragedy. However, he was already outside the building when the pyrotechnics ignited the flammable sound insulation in the ceilings and walls surrounding the stage.

Knott was a patrolman whose beat was Cowesett Avenue South, and it was routine for him to stop at the nightclub on busy evenings to check the parking situation, cash area, and bathrooms. Patrolman Anthony Bettencourt was the detail cop inside the club that night.

Above and below: The Station nightclub memorial wall at
The Rock Junction, Coventry, RI. Photos by Marilyn Bellemore.

Knott arrived around 10:30 p.m., and just as Great White was taking the stage, about a half hour later, he received a phone call that his digital camera was needed at a domestic disturbance across town.

"As soon as I walked out the door, Officer Bettencourt called over the radio to send the fire department," explained Knott, who then radioed dispatch and walked toward the building.

But, as he opened the doors, a stampede of exiting people knocked Knott over the outside railing, and he landed on his back on the hood of a car.

Knott got up and began using his baton to break windows and help people out of the building as the smoke grew thicker.

"It was extremely graphic and tragic, but everyone there was doing something to help," he said.

Patrolman Bettencourt made the first emergency call. He asked the West Warwick police dispatcher to send the fire department and reported there were already people trapped inside the burning building. At least four other people at The Station called 911 for help, within the next minute.

At 11:10 pm the West Warwick Fire Department (WWFD) dispatched a standard structural fire response which included the three closest engine companies, the ladder truck, and an ambulance, all under the command of the battalion chief. Through 911 calls and radio traffic from the scene, the WWFD fire alarm operator upgraded the initial assignment to include the town's remaining engine company.

Brian Butler, a cameraman for WPRI-TV Providence, caught the horrific fire on videotape from its inception. The eight-plus minute tape is now viewable on YouTube. Quickly spreading smoke, and blockage of many of the exit doors, made escape impossible for all too many of the patrons.

This fire occurred just three days after a nightclub stampede at E2 in Chicago which took the lives of 21 people, and Butler was at The Station to tape a segment on nightclub safety. Jeffrey Derderian, a WPRI-TV news reporter and co-owner of the nightclub, was to cover the story. Because Derderian was doing a piece on his own property, WPRI-TV was later cited for conflict of interest.

Knott explained, "We weren't sure what happened. We treated it as a crime scene, secured it, and maintained the evidence."

The Cowesett Inn, diagonally across from the nightclub, became a triage site. John Barylick, a lawyer who wrote, "Killer Show: The Station Nightclub Fire, America's Deadliest Rock Concert," and spoke at Barnes and Noble Bookstore in Warwick on October 11, 2012, said only four people who made their way out of the building that night died.

"I hope, God forbid, if I'm ever in a situation [like the Station nightclub fire]," said Barylick, "my instincts will be to do the right thing. We are our own best fire marshals."

Knott said that it's hard to train people for what they can't see or hear, but, as a police safety officer, they're trained to react to a situation, big or small.

"When things get tense or chaotic, we're trained to stay focused and calm and fulfill whatever mission we're there for," he noted. "We don't have the luxury to walk away."

Calls for Mutual Assistance reached as far as Connecticut, and firefighters from throughout the state responded with ambulances and other apparatus.

The Station nightclub fire resulted in the deaths of 100 people and injured about 230 others through burns, trampling, and smoke inhalation.

Sign at the entrance to the butterfly gardens at Roger Williams Park Zoo in Providence, RI, dedicated to those people affected by The Station nightclub fire. Photo by Marilyn Bellemore.

Thursday, November 2, 2000
YOU CAN GET YOUR 'FIXX' AT THE STATION TOMORROW

– Marilyn Bellemore, Daily Times Staff Reporter

FANS OF THE FIXX are in luck. The band, with all its original members, will play The Station, 211 Cowesett Ave., tomorrow night.

During the 1990s, Cy Curnin (lead vocals), Adam Woods (drums), Jamie West-Oram (guitar), and Rupert Greenall (keyboards) took a brief hiatus for commitments like marriage and children. However, they are now back in full swing.

"We took time off for domestic things between 1991 and 1995 when everything was grunge," said Curnin. "The only thing different about our music now is there's a bit more maturity behind it. Our audiences have grown. I think it's good for the audience to see the band is still active, still vibrant when we play, because we're much more of a live animal. We're having as much fun now as we ever had."

The Fixx got its start in London in 1980 and signed on with MCA in 1981. Its 1982 debut gold album, *Shuttered Room*, produced the hits "Red Skies" and

The Fixx.

"Stand or Fall" and spent more than a year on the American charts.

Reach the Beach, from 1983, eventually went double platinum. The songs "One Thing Leads to Another" and "Saved by Zero," from this album, helped the band make its mark in the rock music world.

Another gold album, *Phantoms*, brought the 1985 hit "Our We Ourselves." Over the years, The Fixx released more albums.

Presently, *The Ultimate Fixx Collection*, somewhat of a greatest hits CD, is available on Hip-O/MCA Records. And the band is now working on a yet-to-be named album.

Curnin explained that the band, which is now recording in New York, hopes to complete its latest project by late spring 2001.

"We're doing 15 gigs on this tour," said Curnin of tomorrow night's show. "Texas, California, Seattle, and West Warwick. We extend the arrangements and get deep on the album cuts and the well-known hits. We'll be playing all the hits and more—a home-grown mix."

The lead vocalist said The Fixx was last in the area about two years ago for an appearance on WFNX in Boston. And, although the band first became popular in the 1980s, its fan base continues to broaden.

"We are physically an '80s band, (but) we've grown into being a current band," explained Curnin. "We're not big on pigeonholes. It was you had to go out and prove yourself as a live act. Good format radio stations are still having a lot of success playing '80s music. We have a few new followers who were too young to come (and see us) the first time around."

With The Fixx and Kristen Trahan Cole, then editor of *The Kent County Daily Times,* on November 3, 2000. Photo by Dave Cole.

And, what has Curnin never been asked that he'd like to answer?

"Sometimes bands are only in it for a quick buck," added Curnin. "We're not. We're a good live act and that's the bread and butter of our survival. There's more of a need to get out and about. There's a sense of community when a band comes out. It brings the fans together. We're more of an out-there band."

White Collar Criminals and Katrin open for The Fixx tomorrow night. Tickets are $13 in advance and $15 the day of the show.

"Passion is passion," said Curnin. "We're extremely lucky to be doing the one thing we love to do. That's success, really."

The Fixx drew one of the biggest crowds I'd ever seen at The Station. I wore a white crop top and maroon leather pants because that was the look in those days. The dance floor was hot and sweaty, the lights dim, and the music blaring. I was with my editor, Kristen, and her boyfriend, Dave. When the high-energy show was over, Cy Curnin and the guys set up a table and signed just about every type of Fixx memorabilia that fans handed them.

Still an active band, check www.thefixx.com, for more information.

Above and below, memorial to Ty Longley, guitarist for Great White, who died in The Station nightclub fire, at the site on Cowesett Avenue. Photos by Marilyn Bellemore.

Thursday, January 18, 2001
COME ON FEEL THE NOISE WITH QUIET RIOT AT THE STATION JANUARY 25

– Marilyn Bellemore, Daily Times Staff Reporter

IF THE LIST OF SHOWS at The Station has read like a 'where are they now' of popular '80s bands, then 2001 continues the trend with an appearance by the legendary rockers Quiet Riot.

The group will play at The Station, 211 Cowesett Ave., on Jan. 25.

"The Station show is our first show of the year and we're definitely pumped," said Kevin DuBrow, lead singer. "We're going to be dressing up in leather, studs, and glittery, glamorous stuff. We never embraced the alternative fashions. We've always been about dressing up on stage and giving people something to see as well as something to hear."

Quiet Riot's latest album is called *Guilty Pleasures*. DuBrow said he began writing the lyrics in August 2000. So far, the band has recorded seven of the songs and will go back to Rumbo Studios in Canoga Park, Calif. on Feb. 19 to finish the last five tracks.

Quiet Riot.

"There is no doubt this is the best the band has sounded since *Metal Health,* and the quality of the songwriting surpasses everything we've written in a long time," said drummer Frankie Banali. "I couldn't be happier or more excited!"

"The album will be released on June 1, 2001 and will coincide with the summer tour," explained Du-Brow. "Lyric wise, this is my baby. I try to write a lyric that I felt went with the music. I hope that we got better. We didn't try to re-invent the wheel with this album.

"Some of it sounds like our old stuff because we want to be loyal to our fans. We made a few left turns to get some expansion on what we originally sounded like. It's hard rock, heavy metal. Very much in the vein of what people know Quiet Riot to do. We try to get better at it in the process and add some more originality to it."

Quiet Riot got its start in Los Angeles in 1985 as a standard hard rock group. DuBrow was lead vocalist with Randy Rhoads on guitar, Drew Forsyth on drums, and Kelly Garni on bass. Their first album, *Quiet Riot*, was released in 1977. *Quiet Riot 2* followed in 1978.

Rudy Sarzo replaced Garni, and Banali replaced Forsyth. Carlos Cavazo was added as a second guitarist alongside Rhoads in 1987.

Quiet Riot was on hiatus in early 1980. There were plans to regroup in May 1982, but Rhoads was killed in a plane accident in March 1982.

The group reformed in October 1982 with DuBrow, Sarzo, Banali, and Cavazo.

The 1983 *Metal Health* was the first heavy metal album to reach #1 on the Billboard charts and go on to sell more than 10 million albums. With it came the hits "Cum On Feel the Noize" and "Metal Health."

Unlike other bands that made their mark in the 1980s, Quiet Riot enjoys being associated with that period in music history.

"It was a great, fun decade," noted DuBrow. "And, I'm grateful to have a career in the business.

I'm proud of our heritage. I didn't understand a lot about the '90s music. I think this decade is off to a great start. Our band is designed to elicit a strong response from people. We are entertainers. We're not here to give you a message. I can't stand anything more than going to see a movie and it being lousy. We're conscious of people walking away and being disappointed. We don't want (them) to say 'that sucked.'"

DuBrow said Quiet Riot last played at The Station two years ago. He said he remembers playing in Rhode Island many times and recalls opening for Black Sabbath in Providence in the 1980s.

"I remember all our shows in Rhode Island," added DuBrow. "We get a great response and, in the process, we enjoy ourselves. After the Black Sabbath show I remember taking a walk with Frankie (Banali). We wanted to get something to eat."

DuBrow invites all his fans to The Station to join them for a great night. He said they're going to play a lot of music from *Metal Health* and three songs from the upcoming album although he's unsure of which ones.

"We work on new material at the soundchecks, and we perform it at night to see how it works with an audience," DuBrow added.

Next Thursday's performance will include Cavazo

on guitar, Sarzo on bass, and Banali on drums.

"The fans in Rhode Island have been very good to us over the years," said Banali. "I enjoy playing The Station in West Warwick. It's a funky rock club, and the audience is just nuts. I love that!"

Tickets are $11 in advance and $13 the day of the show. Opening acts are Powderburnt and $kyhigh.

Although the Quiet Riot episode on VH1's Behind the Music aired in July 1999, I didn't see it until after I did this interview. I therefore had no preconceived notions about the hardships that they, as musicians, had faced, or knew much about their crazy lifestyles.

Kevin DuBrow, Quiet Riot's lead singer, was found dead of a cocaine overdose on November 25, 2007. DuBrow had a reputation for being arrogant and a troublemaker among his peers in the music world. But, I found him to be enthusiastic. He probably would have talked all night, if I had let him.

In September 2010, Frankie Banali, the drummer, announced a new lineup for Quiet Riot, with Mark Huff as lead vocalist. On January 12, 2012, Huff was fired from the band just as he was to undergo brain surgery and was replaced for upcoming gigs with Keith St. John.

For future Quiet Riot shows, go to www. officialquietriot.com.

The Aftermath

*"But February made me shiver With every paper
I'd deliver Bad news on the doorstep I couldn't
take one more step"*
                    – Don McLean, "American Pie"

Four days after the fire, thousands of mourners paid their respects at a memorial service at St. Gregory the Great Church on Cowesett Avenue in Warwick. Governor Donald Carcieri declared a moratorium on pyrotechnic displays at venues that hold fewer than 300 people.

Attorneys for the Derderians said that the brothers did not give Great White permission to use pyrotechnics although band members claimed they were given permission.

"The Station nightclub fire occurred without warning at a venue crowded with unsuspecting patrons in a densely populated area of Rhode Island. It caused immediate

69

Major Mark Knott of the West Warwick Police Department.

mass casualties and fatalities beyond the experience of the local response community," according to the The Station Club Fire After-Action Report distributed by the Governor's Office.

"The event provided a thorough test of the plans, procedures, equipment, personnel, and capabilities that make up the Rhode Island emergency management system. The lessons learned will help authorities better prepare for future cataclysmic events, regardless of their cause," the report went on to say.

"It has raised awareness to overcrowding and recognizing your exits from a management perspective," said Major Mark Knott of the West Warwick Police Department, who was at the nightclub when the fire ignited. "(It was) the premiere that forced a lot of change."

A breakdown of the aftermath:

- Daniel Biechele, the group's tour manager, who set off the pyrotechnics, pleaded guilty to one hundred counts of involuntary manslaughter; sentenced to 15 years' imprisonment, of which 11 years were suspended; thus, four years "to serve." He was paroled after serving 16 months.

- Michael Derderian pleaded *nolo contendere* to 100 counts of involuntary manslaughter; sentenced to 15 years' imprisonment, of which 11 years were suspended; thus, four years "to serve." He was paroled after serving 27 months.

- Jeffrey Derderian pleaded *nolo contendere* to 100 counts of involuntary manslaughter; sentenced to 10 years' imprisonment, all of which were suspended. He was ordered to perform 500 hours of community service.

- Jack Russell, lead singer for Great White and Daniel Biechele's employer, and Denis Larocque, West Warwick fire marshal, were never charged.

Dave Kane, 64, father of the youngest fire victim, Nicholas O'Neill, said, "People that should have been charged, weren't. Dan Biechele should never have been charged for all that he was. The whole thing was about a lack of justice for these families. The reason these people were treated this way is they were considered to be the great unwashed. (Many of them) were rock 'n rollers, they had tattoos, had no political clout, blue collar workers. Frankly, they were just dismissed by the powers that be."

Kane, who was a well known radio talk show host in Rhode Island for decades, and one of the most outspoken advocates for a victims' memorial at The Station fire site, said he didn't mind getting painted as a crackpot.

Tributes to Nicholas O'Neill and others at The Station site in West Warwick.
Photo by Marilyn Bellemore.

Crosses at the Station nightclub site in memory of the victims. The large one in the center is dedicated to Mike Gonsalves, a disc jockey with WHJY radio for more than 17 years, known as The Doctor of heavy metal. Photo by Marilyn Bellemore.

Angel at The Station nightclub memorial in St. Ann Cemetery in Cranston.
Photo by Marilyn Bellemore.

He wanted to use his experience in the media to help people.

"If a child of an elected official, the governor, or a congressman had been in there, if that club had been on the East Side (of Providence), it would have been an entirely different deal," noted Kane. "These people were protecting themselves. They didn't want the fire marshal on the stand because everyone would have done time."

- In February 2008, Providence television station WPRI-TV made an out-of-court settlement of $30 million as a result of the claim that Brian Butler, the cameraman inside the nightclub, was obstructing escape and not helping patrons exit the building.

- In late March 2008, JBL Speakers settled out of court for $815,000. The company was accused of using flammable foam inside its speakers, yet denied any wrongdoing.

- Anheuser-Busch offered $5 million; McLaughlin & Moran (Anheuser-Busch's distributor) offered $16 million.

- Clear Channel Broadcasting offered $22 million.

Tiny angel at The Station nightclub site on Cowesett Avenue.
Photo by Marilyn Bellemore.

- Home Depot and insulation company, Polar Industries, also made a settlement offer of $5 million. Sealed Air Corporation agreed to pay $25 million as settlement (it made the sound-proofing foam). American Foam Company, who sold the insulation to the nightclub, agreed to a settlement of $6.3 million.

- The State of Rhode Island and the town of West Warwick agreed to pay $10 million as settlement.

- Michael and Jeffrey Derderian offered $813,000 in settlement which will be covered by their insurance plan due to the brothers having bankruptcy protection from lawsuits.

- Great White offered $1 million in settlement to survivors and victims' relatives, the maximum allowed under the band's insurance plan.

Victoria Potvin Eagan, a Station fire survivor and vice president of The Station Fire Memorial Foundation, said obviously it was a horrible tragedy. She had gone to the nightclub with friends, like so many people that evening, to hear Great White, a national act.

"Something to remember is a lot of people were there to have a good time. We loved music," said Eagan. "There have been some amazing friendships and a sense of family we have created over the past nine and a half years, that did not exist before. That's the positive thing people need to take out of this. There have been so many stories of survival and triumph."

Thursday, February 15, 2001
WARRANT SERVES UP 'CHERRY PIE' AT STATION

— Marilyn Bellemore, Daily Times Staff Reporter

THESE GUYS HOPE to be remembered for putting on a good show. And, they say that The Station is the place to do just that.

Warrant, which produced the hits "Heaven," "Sometimes She Cries," "Uncle Tom's Cabin," and "Cherry Pie," will play at the club at 211 Cowesett Ave. tomorrow night.

"We always have a blast at The Station," said Erik Turner, an original guitar player with the band. "It's our third or fourth time playing there. At the end of the night, everyone is hot, sweaty, and exhausted. It's like good sex. We want everyone to come to The Station, and when you think of Warrant, think 'party'."

Considered one of the most popular "big hair" bands of its time, Warrant was named by former drummer Max Asher. How he came up with the name, Turner said he has no clue.

Today, the band includes two original members—Jani Lane, lead singer, and Jerry Dixon, bassist.

"We sound better than ever," said Turner. "This is the best lineup we've ever had. We've been called a lot of different things but we're a melodic, hard rock band. We were always called an '80s band, and I think it kind of set in. But, technically, we released one album in the '80s and five in the '90s."

Turner said he got his start as a guitar player when he was 15 years old. He took lessons, but not for long.

"I had friends who played guitar and learned a lot of stuff by picking it up from them," he explained. "The music I liked from the '70s and '80s was Led Zeppelin, Aerosmith, ACDC, Kiss, Ted Nugent, and on and on."

Warrant.

The late Janie Lane, lead singer of Warrant on left, with Rich Antonelli, musician with the former local band $kyhigh and The Station's website designer, outside the nightclub on February 15, 2001.
Photo courtesy of Rich Antonelli.

In July 1984, when Turner was 20 years old, he formed Warrant. Two months later, he was joined by Dixon.

"Jerry and I met when we were playing the local circuit and all the different clubs in the Los Angeles area," explained Turner.

Lane joined Warrant as lead singer in 1986. The band's first album, *Dirty Rotten Filthy Stinking Rich*, was released in 1989.

"Our first record 'Heaven' sold almost a million copies as a single," noted Turner. "And, the album sold three million copies."

Also on the album was "Sometimes She Cries."

In 1990, came Warrant's next release *Cherry Pie*.

Warrant in 2011 with Robert Mason (formerly of Lynch Mob) on lead vocals.

It included the hit of the same name as well as "Uncle Tom's Cabin" and "I Saw Red."

The band recorded its last studio album, *Belly to Belly*, in 1996 and has nine records in its catalog.

Turner said that Warrant has never stopped playing, although Lane quit the band for six months in 1993.

"In 1997, I took a hiatus for a year," explained Turner. "I opened a juice and coffee bar in California. Then, I gave it up because I love being in a band, making music, and playing guitar."

The Los Angeles native said he also designs websites on the side and is definitely Internet literate. He always checks out the ones dedicated to Warrant.

"We've been writing songs for a new CD," said Turner. "We have eight recorded. Hopefully, the release date will be sometime this summer. Jani is the main songwriter although I've written some."

During its big hair days, Warrant played many times in Providence and shared the bill with Poison and Mötley Crüe. Now, the band plays five or six shows a month and hope to be on the road all during summer 2001.

The newest band members, Billy Morris (guitar) and Mike Fasano (drummer), joined Warrant in 2000.

Videocaps from Warrant's music video for "Cherry Pie."

"I just think we're very fortunate to have such great fans," noted Turner. "And, that we've been working for the last 12 years. That's a blessing."

Tickets for Warrant are $15 in advance and $17 the day of the show. Opening acts are $kyhigh and Lunar FX.

Initially, I was scheduled to interview Jani Lane, the lead singer. Instead, the interview was with Erik Turner, guitarist.

It's hard to forget the MTV video for "Cherry Pie," Warrant's most popular tune. Bobbie Brown, the model/actress in the red halter top, met Jani during its filming and married him a couple of months later. They divorced after two years, but the video remains a timeless classic.

Jani left Warrant for the last time in 2008. He was lead singer for Great White on its summer 2010 tour, replacing Jack Russell who was having health issues. Jani died from acute alcohol poisoning on August 11, 2011.

Warrant is still performing. The latest information about the band can be found at warrantrocks.com.

Thursday, March 29, 2001
THE ALARM SOUNDS AT THE STATION
– Marilyn Bellemore, Daily Times Staff Reporter

WHEN YOU THINK OF ROCK MUSIC, Wales is not necessarily the first place that comes to mind.

Perhaps the most critically acclaimed rock band in the history of that country will make its first appearance in West Warwick, and lead singer Mike Peters promises a personal touch for those in attendance.

The Alarm, whose hits include "The Stand," "68 Guns," "Rain in the Summertime," and "Spirit of '76," will play at The Station, 211 Cowesett Ave., on April 5.

As Peters put it, "there was no band that really flew the flag and became symbolic with the nation like The Alarm."

Although the band split up in 1991, Peters continues to keep The Alarm's music alive through the 10-year-old website www.thealarm.com. Last year, he bought the rights to all The Alarm records from EMI and reissued them to the website.

Complete Collection: The Alarm 2000 is now available as a nine CD box set for $168. To date, more than 10,000 copies have been sold.

The Alarm.

"Everyone who buys a box set can choose their favorite album song. Then, I record it personally for them with an acoustic guitar," explained Peters, a native of Rhyl, Wales. "They can choose a spoken dedication at the beginning, and they can have it played at their wedding, funeral, or birthday celebration. It's amazing what I have to do. I speak the dedication of their funeral. This is Mike Peters of The Alarm speaking... (person's name) is still going out with 'A Blaze of Glory'."

Peters has a mobile studio from which he works. If someone wants a song dedication, they can have it recorded in advance or at The Alarm concert they are attending.

At next Thursday's performance at The Station, fans will have the opportunity to hear their recording live on stage.

"People love it," noted Peters. "They bring all their friends to hear it. It commemorates that moment for the rest of their lives. The music of The Alarm has been alive for 20 years now and, with or without the band, the fans have kept that music alive. I feel, when you put the box set together, the fans should be recognized on an individual basis. Originally, I was going to do it for a short period, but the feedback was so immense from the first few (that) I decided to keep it going. The fans were getting a lot from it, and I was learning a lot from the songs, too.

"When you realize the fans have used a piece of your soundtrack, one of the songs, to the most momentous occasion in their lives, it's a very humbling experience to know it."

Peters has been singing for 25 years and is the key songwriter for The Alarm. He said his lyrics are mainly autobiographical. It was a concert by a now legendary rock band that first got him interested in music.

"After seeing the Sex Pistols in 1976 in Chester, England, just over the border (from Wales), they changed my life," noted Peters, who was 17 at the time. "I thought being in a band you had to play 30 minute guitar solos. Then, along came the Sex Pistols, and it made you realize you could express yourself with two or three chords and a couple of words."

Peters started a band called Seventeen in 1978. He said he twiddled away with it until it became The Alarm in 1981.

The band first came to America in 1983 when it opened for U2 on the "War" tour. The Alarm song "The Stand" impressed radio listeners. "68 Guns" was the band's first UK hit, and it made the Top 20 in September 1983.

The band's debut album *Declaration* (1984) made it to the Top Five in its first week of release.

The Alarm's release *Strength* (1985) produced the hit "Spirit of '76." At this time, The Alarm made history playing the first global satellite concert—called Spirit of '86—to 26,000 fans at the University of California at Los Angeles and screened live on MTV worldwide.

The third album *Eye of the Hurricane* (1987) included the hit "Rain in the Summertime." The band put out two more albums *Change* (1989) and *Raw* (1991).

Then, on June 30, 1991, during the final night of the "Raw" tour, Peters announced the band was splitting up.

Although The Alarm makes it first appearance in West Warwick next Thursday night, it is not new to the state.

"One of our earliest gigs was at the Living Room in 1983 in Providence," recalled Peters. "We played in Rhode Island on every tour from 1983 to 1991. I played an acoustic gig four or five years ago. But, this is the first time The Alarm's music has been heard in America in 10 years with an electric band."

The lead singer is the only original band member who will play at The Station next Thursday. Expect to hear James Stevenson (Generation X and Gene Loves Jezebel) on guitar, Steve Grantley (Stiff Little Fingers) on drums, and Richard Llewellyn, a 26-year-old Alarm fan, on bass.

Tickets for The Alarm are $7 in advance and $9 on the day of the show.

The Alarm.

"My philosophy in life is to say 'yes' to everything now, and worry about fitting it in later," added Peters. "That's why I'm in three bands (The Alarm, Colour Sound, and Dead Men Walking) and make records personally for every single fan. I'm probably a bit insane on the side."

More than a decade ago, when I wrote this article, The Alarm was considered the most popular Welsh band of all time. And, that still holds true today. In the recent book "Wales Since 1939" (2012) by Martin Johnes, the claim is made that The Alarm personified culture trends within the country, and therefore qualifies for a place in the contemporary history of Wales.

Part of the band's staying power is attributed to Mike Peters' dedication to his fans. What I learned from speaking with him is that he remains approachable, and that he keeps coming up with innovative ideas that appeal to this fanbase.

The Alarm has an extensive website (www. thealarm.com) which is updated daily with concert information.

The Memorial/
Ten Years Later

"Now for ten years we've been on our own
And moss grows fat on a rollin' stone"
— Don McLean, "American Pie"

AFTER NEARLY TEN YEARS of waiting and wondering if a permanent memorial to the fire victims would be erected on the land where The Station nightclub once stood, Raymond J. Villanova, 74, land owner, donated it to The Station Fire Memorial Foundation. The announcement was made on September 28, 2012.

This decision came just a week after Dave Kane, 64, of Johnston, suggested the state take the land by eminent domain. Kane, whose son, Nicholas O'Neill, was the youngest fire victim, said, "Once it became clear that the state was serious about taking the land, suddenly, Villanova had this *'come to Jesus'* moment and decided he was going to hand over the land. I couldn't understand it, and, still, I can't understand why he delayed it so long. He got vilified."

At the site of The Station nightclub fire in West Warwick.
Photo by Marilyn Bellemore.

A memorial for fire victims from Warwick. Photo by Marilyn Bellemore.

When Kane was on the board of The Station Fire Memorial Foundation, he said he had conversations with Dan McKiernan, Villanova's attorney, who told him Villanova was going to donate the land. He wasn't able to do so at the time, because the land was in escrow, and he was being sued in the fire.

Then, when it was announced that a memorial was being put in Warwick in honor of 10 victims from that city in September 2012, "and it was referred to as a satellite memorial. It pissed me off," said Kane. "It was the first step away from this land."

On October 20, 2012, the Warwick memorial to The Station nightclub fire victims was unveiled. Nine of the residents' names are inscribed in a granite slab that sits atop a 28-foot diameter brick circular plaza. One victim's mother didn't want her daughter memorialized separately on the slab from all the 100 who died in the fire, so chose not to have her name listed. Around the exterior of the circle are 100 8-by-8 inch bricks with the names of every person whose life was taken.

Victoria Potvin Eagan, 37, of West Warwick, a survivor and vice president of The Station Fire Memorial Foundation, said the donation of the land by Villanova was a goal they were working toward for 9 years. It happened after the lawsuits were final, and that Villanova wanted it to go to the right entity to make the memorial happen, she said.

Plaque at the memorial for fire victims in Warwick.
Photo by Marilyn Bellemore.

"I'm very pleased and happy that he finally reached out to us," said Eagan, a co-founder and past president of The Station Family Fund. "He always intended it to be a memorial and waited for the right time."

In March 2003, just a month after the fire, a plot of land was dedicated at St. Ann Cemetery in Cranston for a memorial to the 100 fire victims. Four years later, the monument was completed. This consists of a 13-foot tall angel surrounded by the names of each individual who perished in the fire. The Diocese of Providence also offered burial for victims at no charge to help lessen emotional or financial burdens on families. Twenty-six individuals were buried at St. Ann Cemetery, with seven at the memorial site.

Eagan explained that the original design for the memorial that will be put at The Station site, was voted on five or six years ago. The unveiling of the final design is scheduled to take place on February 17, 2013 at the 10-year anniversary service. It's scaled back a bit for ease of permanent maintenance in the future. It was designed by Steven Greenleaf, a landscape architect, and Tom Viall, who was touched by the tragedy, Eagan said. The plan is for the memorial to be completed in 12 to 18 months.

"Our big goal is not going to be a huge expense," added Eagan. "A lot of labor and materials are being donated. A least a couple of million is needed for maintenance. We'll be having many fundraisers over the next couple of years."

Tribute at The Station site to Dina Ann DeMaio who was a bartender at the nightclub. Photo by Marilyn Bellemore.

Major Mark Knott of the West Warwick Police Department, who was at The Station on the night of the fire, drives past the site several times a day.

"A properly designed tribute and memorial to the victims would be a lot more fitting than what is there now," said Knott.

The Station Fire Memorial Foundation plans to bury relics like teddy bears and photos that were left at the site in a time capsule at the future memorial.

Thursday, July 26, 2001
THE KINKS' DAVE DAVIES BRINGS 'A ROCK 'N' ROLL FANTASY' TO THE STATION

- Marilyn Bellemore, Daily Times Staff Reporter

IN **1964,** the legendary Kinks recorded its first hit single "You Really Got Me." Dave Davies was just 17-years-old and the lead guitar player.

The group went on to produce a string of favorites including "All Day and All of the Night," "Lola," "A Rock 'N' Fantasy," "Sunny Afternoon," and "Come Dancing."

More than three decades later, The Kinks are doing temporary things, but Dave Davies is still going strong. His self-titled band will be at The Station at 211 Cowesett Ave. on Aug. 2.

"I'm really excited about it. My current release *Rock Bottom* is a live recording from the Bottom Line Club in New York," said Davies. "More current releases will be available at the gig. But, *Rock Bottom* is a big representation of the show. I do kind of hard rock. I'll be playing favorite Kinks that I like. It will be a mix."

The Dave Davies Band includes Jim Laspesa on drums, Dave Jenkins on bass, Jonathan Lea on second guitar, and Kristian Hoffman on keyboards.

The Kinks' Dave Davies.

Davies described the sound as much more raunchy and heavy now, but at the same time there are some lighter more reflective songs.

"Ray and I have been talking about a reunion. We might do something, but we're not sure what it will be," explained Davies about his brother Ray Davies, The Kinks' lead singer. "But, The Kinks never really broke up. In 1995/96, we went into hiatus. Last tour Ray did some shows. I did some solo recording. Obviously, we want to get back to doing something."

For the rest of the year, Davies plans to promote his band. Prior to the West Warwick show, the group will play in Pennsylvania and New Jersey.

In September and October, it will do a five-week European tour and return to the United States in the new year to play more music.

"New York and Massachusetts have big strongholds for The Kinks and the Dave Davies Band," said Davies. "West Warwick is kind of like Massachusetts, and Boston has always been a big fan base over the years."

Davies said his lyrics are inspired by a spiritual quest and focus on three or four themes. Some are reflective of his working class background.

"'Unfinished Business' is really a song about unfulfillment and reaching my goals," he explained. "I'm not sure yet (what those are). At the moment, I want to keep playing and advancing as a spiritual being.

More important for me is to be successful on the spiritual journey."

Spiritual Journey is also a link on Davies' website www.davedavies.com. It contains information from astrologers and spiritual teachers. It includes "gems" from all the great teachers. Psychic mediums have contributed to the site.

"I like to spend time talking to people," said Davies. "I think that's where the future is... Encompassing spiritual information is energy. Music is energy. It really fascinates me. A lot of barriers are breaking down."

The Kinks' Dave Davies.

The United Kingdom resident, who also resides in Los Angeles, said he doesn't have much time to read, but he can always fit in a good movie.

"I love trashy movies — not trashy novels," explained Davies. "That's how I like to relax. I'll watch anything... Tim Burton, *Ed Wood, Ben Hur.*"

Tickets for the Dave Davies Band are $12 in advance and $14 on the day of the show.

"I love the area," added Davies about next Thursday's show. "I've always enjoyed playing the Northeast."

I was too young to remember the release of "Lola," but old enough to recall "Come Dancing."

On June 30, 2004, Davies suffered a serious stroke. He is said to have recovered enough to play guitar, talk, and walk. Davies later said he feels it happened so that he would slow down.

His latest CD is called Hidden Treasures (2011), a compilation of the singles and unreleased tracks that Davies had recorded for his previously unreleased first solo album. It includes various songs from Kinks B-sides.

In Memory of...

Louis S. Alves
Kevin Anderson
Stacie Angers
Christopher Arruda
Eugene Avilez
Tina Ayer
Karla Bagtaz
Mary H. Baker
Thomas Barnett
Laureen Beauchaine
Steven T. Blom
William Christopher Bonardi, III
Kristine Carbone
Richard A. Cabral, Jr.
William W. Cartwright
Edward B. Corbett, III
Michael Cordier
Alfred Crisostomi
Robert Croteau

Lisa D'Andrea
Matthew P. Darby
Dina Ann DeMaio
Albert A. DiBonaventura
Christina DiRienzo
Kevin J. Dunn
Lori K. Durante
Edward Everett Ervanian
Thomas Fleming
Rachael K. Florio-DePietro
Mark A. Fontaine
Daniel Fredrickson
Mark Fresolo
James C. Gahan
Melvin Gerfin, Jr.
Laura L. Gillett
Charline E. Gingras-Fick
Michael J. Gonsalves
James F. Gooden, Jr
Derek Gray
Pamela Gruttadauria
Skott C. Greene
Scott Griffith
Bonnie L. Hamelin
Jude Henault
Andrew Hoban
Abbie L. Hoisington

Memorial at St. Ann Cemetery in Cranston for the fire victims.
Photo by Marilyn Bellemore.

Michael Hoogasian

Sandy Hoogasian

Carlton "Bud" Howorth, III

Eric J. Hyer

Derek Brian Johnson

Lisa Kelly

Tracy F. King

Michael Joseph Kulz

Keith LaPierre

Dale L. Latulippe

Stephen M. Libera

John M. Longiaru

Ty Longley

Andrea Mancini

A calm November day in the butterfly gardens at Roger Williams Park Zoo in Providence, RI. The special place is dedicated to those people affected by The Station nightclub tragedy. Photo by Marilyn Bellemore.

Steven Mancini

Keith A. Mancini

Judith Manzo

Thomas Marion, Jr.

Jeffrey W. Martin

Tammy Mattera-Housa

Kristen McQuarrie

Thomas Medeiros

Samuel J. Miceli, Jr.

Donna M. Mitchell

Leigh Ann Moreau

Ryan M. Morin

Jason Morton

Beth Ellen Mosczynski

Katherine O'Donnell

Nicholas O'Neill

Matthew James Pickett

Carlos L. Pimentel, Sr.

Christopher Prouty

Jeffrey Rader

Teresa Rakowski

Robert L. Reisner, III

Walter Rich

Donald Roderiques

Tracey Romanoff

Tributes at The Station site to Ty Longley, Thomas Medeiros, and Lori K. Durante.
Photo by Marilyn Bellemore.

Joseph Rossi
Bridget Sanetti
Rebecca "Becky" Shaw
Mitchell C. Shubert
Dennis Smith
Victor Stark
Benjamin J. Suffoletto, Jr.
Linda Suffoletto
Shawn Patrick Sweet
Jason Sylvester
Sarah Jane Telgarsky
Kelly Vieira
Kevin R. Washburn
Everett "Tommy" Woodmansee, III
Robert D. Young

Sources

Antonelli, Rich. Interview with Rich Antonelli, musician. Oct. 7, 2012.

Barylick, John. *Killer Show*. University Press of New England, pages 249-251.

Blacklock, Chris. Interview with Chris Blacklock, Station nightclub survivor. Oct. 4, 2012.

Carpenter, Donald. Interview with Donald Carpenter, West Warwick historian. Oct. 20, 2012.

Clarke, Patti. Interview with Patti Clarke, Station nightclub survivor. Oct. 4, 2012.

Eagan, Victoria Potvin. Interview with Victoria Potvin Eagan, Station nightclub survivor. Oct. 22, 2012.

Kane, Dave. Interview with David Kane, father of Station nightclub victim, Nicholas O'Neill. Oct. 21, 2012.

Kilgus, Laura. Station nightclub Memorial, a place of peace. *Rhode Island Catholic*. Oct. 11, 2012.

Knott, Mark. Interview with Major Mark Knott of the West Warwick (RI) Police Department. Oct. 5, 2012.

Lanigan, Tom. Interview with Tom Lanigan, musician, Oct. 15, 2012.

Pawtuxet Valley Preservation and Historical Society. "The Tale of 211 Cowesett Ave."

Petrella, Dean, Interview with Dean Petrella, musician. Oct. 13, 2012.

Report of the Technical Investigation of The Station Nightclub Fire. National Institute of Standards and Technology. fire.nist.gov/bfrlpubs/fire05/PDF/f05032.pdf.

Smith, Amby. When The Station first opened. *Kent County Daily Times*. Feb. 22, 2003.

Smith, Michelle R. Memorial for '03 RI nightclub fire unveiled. newstimes.com. Oct. 20, 2012.

The Station Club Fire After-Action Report. Distributed by the Governor's Office. 2004, pages A6, A10, and 2.

Acknowledgements

THANK YOU to all the people and organizations that helped make this book a reality:

Michelle Carrier-Migliozzi, my former editor at *The Kent County Daily Times*, for saying "yes" when I asked if I could interview the bands that played at The Station nightclub; Chris Blacklock and Patti Clarke for sharing their incredible story of survival and love of rock 'n roll music with me; Major Mark Knott of the West Warwick Police Department for explaining his role as a first responder and public safety officer on the night of fire; Musicians Rich Antonelli, Tom Lanigan, and Dean Petrella for describing fond memories of playing at the nightclub (also, Rich for photos and Tom for ticket copyrights); Dave Kane for recounting the story of his son, Nicholas O'Neill, the youngest fire victim, and his thoughts on the aftermath; Victoria Potvin Eagan, vice president of The Station Fire Memorial Foundation, for depicting her experiences as a fire survivor and involvement as a past president and co-founder of The Station Family Fund. Also, for her positive outlook; Jon Campbell for reviewing the manuscript with me; Local historian Donald Carpenter for recalling West Warwick in days gone by; Diane Plante for continuing to maintain current information about The Station nightclub fire at the Pawtuxet Valley Preservation and Historical Society; West Warwick Public Library reference staff for providing invaluable assistance along the way; and, lastly, to John Teehan and the Merry Blacksmith Press for helping me to keep the memories and music of The Station nightclub alive.

A memorial to The Station nightclub fire victims at the site on
Cowesett Avenue reads "Angels with us."
Photo by Marilyn Bellemore,

Made in the USA
San Bernardino, CA
10 February 2018